Every Body Talk is intended to be an introduction to age appropriate caregiver / child conversations about body safety, child abuse prevention, and ultimately sexual assault prevention. *Every Body Talk* should not be treated as the entirety of a conversation on prevention, but as a starting point and touchstone for ongoing conversations about safety with children. Child protection like sexual abuse and sexual assault prevention is a lifelong conversation and *Every Body Talk* is only the beginning. Use *Every Body Talk* as a method for children to become comfortable with discussing their body parts and their feelings. Recognize that risk of harm can also come from other people and other ways not described in *Every Body Talk*. Take time as you read *Every Body Talk* to let your child ask you questions or to reflect on situations presented. Use examples from the book in real life settings as well to facilitate your lifelong conversations on child protection.

And most importantly, by using this book as a guide for your future conversations, you're accomplishing a major first step in ensuring child safety - that you and your child can discuss anything of concern when it comes to them and their body.

This book is about children feeling good about their bodies and having their voice matter when others interact with them. Treat this book just like any other book - read it over and over again and have excitement and joy while reading it. It may even become one of yours and your child's favorite books to read! We've got lots more examples for you to say during these conversations with your child!

STARTING UP

- Talk about the title and what your child likes about their body.

- Ask your child to identify certain body parts—keep it simple- head, eyes, ears, arms, legs, feet. Give them praise and affirmation (*"That's right! Great job!"*). These exercises will get your child into the idea of thinking about their body and doing so in a positive way.

READING THE STORY

- Ask your child *"How would you tell someone to stop if you felt someone was too close or doing or saying something that you did not like?"*

- After your child shares anything, let them know that they are good and strong and that they are doing the right thing by sharing it with you.

AFTER THE STORY

- It may seem difficult, but it is important to give your child the opportunity to share with you if they have ever felt that someone was too close or has done or said something that felt uncomfortable. Let your child know that whatever they share, telling you was the right thing to do.

- Reinforce with your child the lessons of the book— If someone is not playing nice you can tell them, *"I'm done!"* *"Remember, touching is never a secret."* and you can always say *"That's not something I want to do."* *"Telling someone you trust is a definite must!"*

- Be sure as a caregiver that you and your child have the support you need, especially if your child reveals an experience that causes concern. Please see additional resources for further support erinlevitas.org/resources

Learn more at everybodytalkbook.org

For everyone reading this.
We see you. You are not alone.
You are worthy, valuable and smart.
This book is for you.

To

Lexi, Dylan & Graham

and

Blaine & Nate

We love and adore you - you inspire us, make us better
and make the world a better place because you're in it.

Acknowledgements:

It takes a village and we are thankful for each of you. Lauren Shapiro, C. Quince
Hopkins, Alison D'Alessandro, Adam Rosenberg, LifeBridge Health's Center for Hope,
Chimi Boyd-Keyes, Emily Ladau, Georgia Warner, Nanyamkah Mars, Malia Segal,
Roberta Katz, Debi Howard, Zephan Moses, Marina Scherr, Jesse Jachman, Quebec
Street Friends, Caesha Beeker, Carolyn Rogers, Jennifer Keats Curtis, Amanda Wood,
Praise Saflor, The Erin Levitas Foundation community, our friends and family. All the
organizations and individuals who supported us and this work on this journey.

EVERY BODY TALK

Written by
Matthew Mittleman and Marissa Jachman

Art by
Gabby Correia

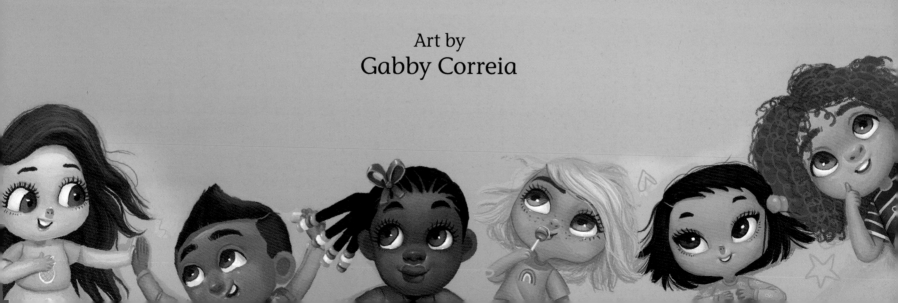

Head, shoulders, knees, and toes.
Eyes, ears, mouth, and nose.
These are some of your body parts, but wait!
There is much more about you to appreciate.

You are unique.
Your body is special to you.
The parts below your waist,
do you know what they're called?
DO YOU NEED A CLUE?

Sometimes people give these parts names like "FLOWER" and "PEEPEE", but these aren't their real names – honestly!

Can you say their real names?

Go on, be a genius...

Those body parts are really called

VAGINA and **PENIS!**

These parts of your body
are very important,
and calling them what they are
is positive reinforcement.

Now that you know their names and can say them loud and clear,
it's time to understand how we care for them so dear.

Your penis, your vagina should be **PROTECTED** with **CARE**. Taking care of them is important, just like combing your hair.

As you get older, you may not need so much help
getting dressed or taking a bath or shower.
And doing these things by yourself can be your new super power.

These parts of your body are **SPECIAL** to you.
Don't share them with everyone
and sometimes we cover them too.

Often we wear something
to keep our parts private - we do!
Like shorts, pants, underwear,
and even diapers too!

As you get ready to start your day,
it's important to understand the
SAFE WAYS to **PLAY**.

16

Sometimes people around you may
want to play differently than you.
So listen up carefully and
we'll tell you what to do.

17

Toys, books, and games are ways to have fun.
But if someone's not playing nice you can tell them,

"I'M DONE!"

If anyone wants to do something that involves any body part,
here's what you can do right from the very start.

If you are touched in a way
that feels not safe or not okay to you,
you can move or walk away and tell them

"THAT'S NOT SOMETHING I WANT TO DO."

I'D LIKE
MY SPACE

If you ever feel unsafe
because someone is too near,

"I'D LIKE MY SPACE,"
is what they can hear.

Whether you're on the moon
or in your room, it can be
any time or anywhere
you can say, or even shout,

**"PLEASE STOP,
GIVE ME SOME AIR."**

If someone wants to touch or see your penis, vagina,
or any body part and you feel unsure or scared, just tell them

"NO! IT'S MY BODY AND IT'S NOT TO BE SHARED!"

If this happens to you, you are not to blame.

This is YOUR body, **"DO NOT TOUCH ME"**, you can exclaim!

Then always tell someone about it who understands you,
so they can help remind you that
saying **"NO"** was the right thing to do.
And if you didn't say "no" that's okay too.

If the situation is switched and someone asks you to touch or see their body part, **STOP** and think about it, you can walk away and listen to your heart.

We respect others' words and their bodies too. So, it's important **NOT** to **TOUCH** others' bodies without permission whether you're in the lunch room or at a zoo.

Others may laugh or tease,
but no matter how they say it.
You must know that touching is

NEVER a SECRET.

Teasing or touching can also happen in different places, you see,
like at a friend's house, a school hallway, a park, or with family.
The person may try to tell you that it's **"JUST A GAME"**,
but it definitely isn't even nearly the same!

There are even times a doctor
may need to check you out.
And you can still ask a loved one
if there's ever any doubt.

29

No matter where you are,
make sure your mind never forgets.
That it's important to follow these
three simple steps:

MY SPACE!

STEP TWO is to say "I'd like my space" loud and clear. And to say it even louder if they don't seem to hear!

STEP ONE is to have pride in your body, you don't have to do what they say. Keeping your body parts yours is how it should stay.

STEP THREE is to tell a grown-up about it – someone you trust. Because telling others about it is a definite must.

So, if you are uncomfortable, worried, or unsure,
remember these 3 steps and you'll have confidence once more.
We want you to know you have control over each body part.
Knowing their real names and the 3 steps is a great start!

If you have more **QUESTIONS**,
seek **SOMEONE** you trust,

ask them, and proceed.

Because having these healthy conversations is positive indeed!

So be proud of your body, your vagina, your penis.
Remember that's what they are called,
whether you live on Earth, Mars, or Venus.

VAGINA

PENIS

34

3 GROWN-UPS I trust and can talk to if there's an emergency. Or if something happened to me that made me happy. Or if something happened that I didn't like or didn't feel safe to me, like gave me butterflies in my tummy, made my heart beat fast, made my legs wobbly or gave me goosebumps.

1

2

3

Resources:
The National Sexual Assault Telephone Hotline | RAINN | www.rainn.org
When you call 800.656.HOPE (4673), you'll to be routed to a local sexual assault service
provider in your area. Trained staff can provide confidential support.
Childhelp National Child Abuse Hotline | www.childhelp.org
1-800-4-A-CHILD (1-800-422-4453) Text, Call or Chat.
The Childhelp National Child Abuse Hotline is open 24/7. All calls are confidential.

100% of profits support sexual assault and sexual abuse prevention.
This has been funded by The Erin Levitas Foundation that envisions a
future with education for youth and young adults to
prevent sexual assault and help survivors heal: erinlevitas.org

Illustrated by Gabby Correia
Book Design by Praise Saflor

Library of Congress Control Number: 2021909304

ISBN: 978-0-578-91136-6